DAVID WENTZ

John Wesley's The Scripture Way of Salvation

Set in Modern Language with Introduction and Suggestions for Group Use

DOING CHRISTIANITY
Pastor David Wentz

Contents

Introduction

by David Wentz

In some churches being saved means answering an altar call or repeating the sinner's prayer. In others it's taking a class, making a promise, or getting baptized. Many define salvation as having a personal relationship with Jesus. For others it's all about trying to be a good person. However they think of it, for most Christians, the point of salvation is getting to heaven.

Getting to heaven is important, of course. And you can't get to heaven unless you're right with God. That happens when we confess our sins, turn toward God, and put our faith in Jesus. When we do that, our sins are forgiven,[1] our guilt is wiped out,[2] and we become children of God.[3] Then when God looks at us, he sees the righteousness of Jesus.[4]

Getting right with God is called justification. Many people

---

[1] *In him we have redemption through his blood, the forgiveness of our trespasses, according to the riches of his grace* (Ephesians 1:7)

[2] *Erasing the record that stood against us with its legal demands. He set this aside, nailing it to the cross.* (Colossians 2:14)

[3] *But to all who received him, who believed in his name, he gave power to become children of God.* (John 1:12)

[4] *For our sake he made him to be sin who knew no sin, so that in him we might become the righteousness of God.* (2 Corinthians 5:21)

think it's the same as being saved.

Not John Wesley. In "The Scripture Way of Salvation," Wesley shows that salvation goes way beyond just getting your sins forgiven and your ticket punched for eternity. Justification is just the beginning. For full salvation, there's a second part. It's sanctification, the journey toward holiness in our hearts and in our lives.

Some think justification is all God requires. Others acknowledge that the Bible tells us to be holy,[5] but they believe it's actually an unrealistic goal that can't be reached until we get to heaven. Still others believe sanctification happens automatically when we are justified.

The problem with all three of these views is that they let Christians off the hook. They all imply that once we accept Jesus as our Savior and have our sins forgiven, then we've checked off God's requirements and we can get on with our lives. That's a big reason why so many Christians seem to be spiritually coasting.

Wesley taught that ordinary Christians can achieve sanctification in this life. We all can reach the place where we are no longer consciously committing any sins and where every thought, word, and action is motivated by love. And he taught that we should actively seek and work toward it. Along with the insistence that Christianity should be an experience of God and not just an intellectual belief, this urging toward holiness was the defining characteristic of the Wesleyan revival. The many Methodist and Wesleyan denominations, the Pentecostal and holiness movements, and the Salvation Army all trace their

_____

[5] *Instead, as he who called you is holy, be holy yourselves in all your conduct.* (1 Peter 1:15)

lineage back to these teachings.

In Wesley's day, which spanned most of the 1700s, his followers believed what he taught fiercely. They lived it out faithfully. They witnessed to it boldly — so much so that they were often violently persecuted by those who felt their own lukewarm faith and pop culture values threatened.

Today millions of people attend the churches descended from the Wesleyan revival, but Wesley's teachings on full salvation are seldom heard. Perhaps this is the reason it's often hard to tell the difference between people who attend those churches and their neighbors who don't go to church at all.

Say again, please?

John Wesley's teachings and writings were clear, logical, and Biblical. They sparked a revival that could not be contained in the established church, and its effects are still felt today.

Wesley's logic, clarity, and Biblical truth are as potent as they ever were. Unfortunately, his 300-year-old English is more and more difficult for modern readers to understand. Wesley was a revival preacher with the best of them. People were often so struck by his words that they cried out and even fell to the ground. Today, the mental effort of interpreting his archaic phrases can rob them of their power.

That's where this book comes in. I've put his words into modern English, while as much as possible maintaining his original structure and style. My goal is not only to help you understand Wesley's points but to give you a sense of what it was like to hear him preach.

I believe Wesley would approve. He wrote, "I design plain truth for plain people:… I labor to avoid all words which are not easy to be understood, all which are not used in common life."[6]

Besides being a powerful revival preacher, Wesley had a genius for organizing those who responded to his messages so they could keep growing in faith and living in holiness. As his movement grew, Wesley gathered fifty-eight of his most important sermons into a book which he published for his lay preachers to read, learn, and then preach in their own words. "The Scripture Way of Salvation" is number forty-three of the fifty-eight. While you can read it straight through, as Wesley's original listeners would have heard it, I've broken it up here into bite-size sections to make it easier to discuss and digest. For scholars and the curious, Wesley's original is included as an appendix.

Radical, man!

As you go through "The Scripture Way of Salvation," you're likely to come across some statements that strike you as unrealistic, if not downright radical. That was John Wesley. These were the things he taught. I can make the language easier to understand, but that doesn't make what he says any easier for our old nature to accept. But isn't the same thing true of Jesus? Wesley just took what Jesus said, clearly explained it,

---

[6] "Preface to the Sermons," from *The Works of John Wesley,* Third American Edition, 1872.

and carried it to its logical conclusion, without the exceptions and excuses we like to make. The result is a whole new way of living.

What would it look like if we were to rediscover this Wesleyan ideal? What would it look like if every local church in every group that traces its heritage back to Wesley were to become known as a place where people are actively trying to live this kind of new life, because they've been given a new birth?

Frankly, we might lose some people, because Wesley's Christianity is not an easy feel-good religion. But if people today are anything like people when this was first written – and I believe they are, because human nature doesn't change – a lot of people would find this type of faith immensely attractive.

Wesley's method for finding spiritual truth

In his Preface to the first collection of sermons he published, Wesley explained his method for finding spiritual truth:[7]

> To candid, reasonable people I am not afraid to lay open what have been the inmost thoughts of my heart. I have thought, *I am a creature of the day, passing through life, as an arrow through the air. I am a spirit come from God, and returning to God: just hovering over the great gulf; till a few moments from now, I am no more seen! I drop into an unchangeable eternity! I want to*

---

[7] "Preface to the Sermons," from *The Works of John Wesley*, Third American Edition, 1872. Language updated.

know one thing, the way to heaven: how to land safe on that happy shore.

God himself has condescended to teach the way. For this very reason he came from heaven. He has written it down in a book! Oh give me that book! At any price, give me the book of God!

I have it! Here is knowledge enough for me. Let me be a man of one book.

Here I am then, far from the busy ways of people. I sit down alone. Only God is here. And in his presence I open and read this book. My purpose: to find the way to heaven.

Is there a doubt concerning the meaning of something I read? Does anything appear unclear or confusing?

I lift up my heart to the Father of lights, praying: *Lord, doesn't your word say, If anyone lacks wisdom, let him ask of God? You give generously and ungrudgingly.*[8] *You said if anyone is willing to do your will, they shall know.*[9] *I am willing! Let me know your will.*

Then I search after and consider parallel passages of scripture, comparing spiritual things with spiritual.[10]

---

[8] *If any of you is lacking in wisdom, ask God, who gives to all generously and ungrudgingly, and it will be given you.* (James 1:5)

[9] *Thus says the Lord, your Redeemer, the Holy One of Israel: I am the Lord your God, who teaches you for your own good, who leads you in the way you should go.* (Isaiah 48:17)

[10] *These things we also speak, not in words which man's wisdom teaches but which the Holy Spirit teaches, comparing spiritual things with spiritual.* (1 Corinthians 2:13 NKJV)

I meditate on it,[11] with all the attention and earnestness of which my mind is capable.

If any doubt still remains, I consult those who are experienced in the things of God, and the writings of those who have gone before.

And what I learn in this way, that is what I teach.

Notes on the Paraphrase

Though one of the most widely read men of his time, John Wesley called himself "a man of one book." That book was the Bible. His sermons are liberally sprinkled with Scripture quotations and allusions.

Wesley read the Bible in Greek, Hebrew, and probably German, but for him the English Bible was the King James Version, translated in 1611. For many modern readers, that seventeenth-century English can be even more difficult than Wesley's eighteenth-century phrasing. So for most Bible references in this paraphrase, I chose either the New Revised Standard Version (NRSV) or the New King James Version (NKJV). Both are clear, accurate translations that trace their literary lineage back to the King James Version used by Wesley. The NRSV is more widely used in Methodist churches, so that was my default translation. In some cases where the NKJV

---

[11] *This book of the law shall not depart out of your mouth; you shall meditate on it day and night, so that you may be careful to act in accordance with all that is written in it. For then you shall make your way prosperous, and then you shall be successful.* (Joshua 1:8)

more closely reflected Wesley's wording, I used that translation and noted it.

For clarity, verses and phrases that are direct quotes from the Bible are placed in italics. The many places where Wesley alluded to Scripture without specifically quoting it are in regular print. All quotes and allusions are end-noted.

Finally, the methodical Wesley commonly used the technique of numbering his paragraphs. I have replaced the numbers with subheadings and divided his long block paragraphs into shorter ones to reflect modern usage.

Suggestions for Group Use

John Wesley wrote "The Scripture Way of Salvation" as a sermon, and this version can certainly be read straight through in that way. However, as with all thought-provoking books, Wesley's words will have the greatest impact on our individual lives and on our churches when we discuss them with others.

That was John Wesley's philosophy. Wesley organized his followers into small groups called "classes" which met weekly, usually in people's homes. Their main purpose was to discuss how they could be better Christians, based on the previous week's sermon, and to hold each other accountable for acting that way. Of course, as part of that they experienced a wonderful, joyful fellowship. In the modern phrase, they were "doing life together."

This book is perfectly suited for that kind of small-group experience. It can be a home group, a coffee shop gathering, or an adult Sunday School class. To facilitate such use, I have broken the material into six parts. Each should take less than fifteen minutes to read. I have also included some suggested discussion questions at the end of each part, to get you started.

How to Lead a Small Group

Small group gatherings are easy. You can meet in the same place every time, or in different people's homes. You can have the same leader every time, or rotate leadership. (Being the leader isn't a big deal. The leader is just the person who reads the discussion questions out loud.) A good time frame is an hour to an hour and a half. The tried and true format goes something like this:

- People arrive, say hello, and perhaps munch on some light refreshments.
- Somebody says a prayer to get things started, asking God to guide the conversation and bless anyone who is missing.
- You catch up on anything left over from last week – especially including any good stories about how the study helped someone during the week.
- You talk about as many of the discussion questions as you have time for. Answer the ones that interest you, or make up your own.
- You set place, time and assignments for the next meeting.
- You share prayer concerns and pray for them.
- You go out and live what you've been talking about.

If anyone was absent, the leader or a designated person should call them within a day. Tell them you missed them, see if anything is wrong, and catch them up on what happened. Don't forget to tell them the details of the next meeting.

Suggested Schedule

Six weeks is a good, non-threatening length of time for most people to commit to a study like this. Here's a suggested schedule.

Week 1: Introduction

Week 2: What Do You Mean by Salvation?

Week 3: What Do You Mean by Faith?

Week 4: The Faith That Makes Us Right With God

Week 5: Two Kinds of Repentence

Week 6: The Faith That Makes Us Holy

* * *

Discussion Questions

(1) Why are you here today?

— What do you hope to gain?

(2) What is your church background, if any?

(3) Do you consider yourself saved?

— If so, what does that mean to you?

— If not, why not?

(4) What have you been taught about what it takes to get to heaven?

(5) "It's often hard to tell the difference between people who attend those churches and their neighbors who don't go to church at all. "

— Is this a good thing or a bad thing?

— Why?

— How far does this statement apply to you?

— If it's a bad thing, what can you do about it?

(6) Does Wesley's method for finding spiritual truth seem

reasonable for modern Christians?

— Why or why not?

1

What Do You Mean by Salvation?

You have been saved through faith. — Ephesians 2:8
(NKJV)

Nothing can be more intricate, complex, and hard to understand than religion, as most people think of it. This is not
only true of the religions followed by the ancient Greeks and
Romans, even many of the wisest of them. It's also true of the
religion of those who were, in some sense, Christians; yes, even
those of great fame in the Christian world, those who seemed
to be pillars of the faith.

Yet how easy to understand, how plain and simple a thing, is
the genuine religion of Jesus Christ — as long as we take it in
its original form, just as it is described in the word of God! It is
exactly suited, by the wise Creator and Governor of the world,
to the weak understanding and narrow capacity of humanity
in our present state. How easy this is to see, both with regard
to the goal it sets, and the way to reach that goal!

1

The goal is, in one word, salvation; the way to reach it, faith.

You can easily see that these two little words, faith and salvation, cover the substance of the entire Bible. You could say they're the meat of the whole Scripture. So it's very important that we take all possible care to avoid any mistake about them, and form a true and accurate judgement concerning both the one and the other.

To do that, let's seriously consider three questions:

1. What is salvation?
2. What is the faith by which we are saved?
3. How are we saved by it?

What is salvation?

Our first question is, what is salvation?

The salvation the Bible speaks of in our text verse is not what many people understand by that word. It deals not just with going to heaven, or eternal happiness. It's not the soul going to paradise,[12] what Jesus called "Abraham's bosom."[13] It's not a blessing which lies on the other side of death in what we call the other world. The very words of our text verse itself put this

---

[12] *He replied, "Truly I tell you, today you will be with me in Paradise."* (Luke 23:43)

[13] *So it was that the beggar died, and was carried by the angels to Abraham's bosom. The rich man also died and was buried.* (Luke 16:22 NKJV)

beyond all question. *You have been saved.*[14] It's not something at a distance. It's a present thing. It's a blessing which, through the free mercy of God, you already possess now.

So salvation could be widely defined as encompassing the entire work of God from the first dawning of grace in the soul to it's final consummation in glory.

If we use this wider definition, salvation includes everything that prepares our souls for faith. People often credit this to natural conscience, but it's actually a work of God's Holy Spirit. Theologians call it "prevenient grace."[15] It includes all the ways the Father draws us: all our desires for God, which, if we yield to them, increase more and more; all that light by which the Son of God *gives light to every man coming into the world,*[16] showing everyone how *to do justice, and to love kindness, and to walk humbly with your God;*[17] and all the times God's Spirit nudges our conscience, as he does in the heart of every person. Of course, most people stifle those nudges as soon as possible. Then after a while they forget, or at least deny, that their conscience ever bothered them at all.

But in our text verse we're only concerned with the aspects of salvation that come by faith: justification, or being counted in good standing with God, and sanctification, or being made holy.

---

[14] *You have been saved through faith.* (Ephesians 2:8 NKJV)

[15] "Prevenient" describes something that precedes or goes before something else, usually with the idea of preparing for what follows.

[16] *That was the true Light which gives light to every man coming into the world.* (John 1:9 NKJV)

[17] *He has told you, O mortal, what is good; and what does the Lord require of you but to do justice, and to love kindness, and to walk humbly with your God?* (Micah 6:8)

What is justification?

Justification is another word for pardon. It means all our sins are forgiven.[18] And that means we are accepted by God. The price paid to procure this for us (called by theologians "the meritorious cause of our justification") is the blood[19] and righteousness[20] of Christ. To say it a little more clearly, it's everything Christ did and suffered for us until he poured out his soul for the transgressors[21] on the cross.

The immediate effects of justification are peace and joy. We sense the peace of God, *peace which surpasses all understanding,*[22] and we find ourselves rejoicing *in hope of the glory of God*[23] with

---

[18] *And when you were dead in trespasses and the uncircumcision of your flesh, God made you alive together with him, when he forgave us all our trespasses.* (Colossians 2:13)

[19] *Whom God put forward as a sacrifice of atonement by his blood, effective through faith. He did this to show his righteousness, because in his divine forbearance he had passed over the sins previously committed.* (Romans 3:25)

[20] *And be found in him, not having a righteousness of my own that comes from the law, but one that comes through faith in Christ, the righteousness from God based on faith.* (Philippians 3:9)

[21] *Therefore I will allot him a portion with the great, and he shall divide the spoil with the strong; because he poured out himself to death, and was numbered with the transgressors; yet he bore the sin of many, and made intercession for the transgressors.* (Isaiah 53:12)

[22] *And the peace of God, which surpasses all understanding, will guard your hearts and your minds in Christ Jesus.* (Philippians 4:7)

[23] *Through whom also we have access by faith into this grace in which we stand, and rejoice in hope of the glory of God.* (Romans 5:2 NKJV)

joy inexpressible and full of glory.[24]

At the same time that we are justified, in that very moment, sanctification begins. In that instant we are *born again, born from above,*[25] *born of the Spirit.*[26] There is a real change in us, as well as a change in our relationship with God. *Our inner nature is being renewed day by day.*[27] We feel that *God's love has been poured into our hearts through the Holy Spirit that has been given to us.*[28]

We feel this love producing love in us for every human being, and especially for the children of God. We feel it expelling the love of the world, the love of pleasure, of ease, of honor, of money, together with pride, anger, self-will, and every other evil temper. In a word, we feel God's love changing our earthly, sensual, devilish mind into the mind which was in Christ Jesus.[29]

---

[24] *Whom having not seen you love. Though now you do not see Him, yet believing, you rejoice with joy inexpressible and full of glory.* (1 Peter 1:8 NKJV)

[25] *Jesus answered him, "Very truly, I tell you, no one can see the kingdom of God without being born from above."* (John 3:3) The Greek word *anothen* at the end of the verse can be translated as "again" or "from above."

[26] *What is born of the flesh is flesh, and what is born of the Spirit is spirit.* (John 3:6)

[27] *So we do not lose heart. Even though our outer nature is wasting away, our inner nature is being renewed day by day.* (2 Corinthians 4:16)

[28] *And hope does not disappoint us, because God's love has been poured into our hearts through the Holy Spirit that has been given to us.* (Romans 5:5)

[29] *"For who has known the mind of the Lord so as to instruct him?" But we have the mind of Christ.* (1 Corinthians 2:16)

Sin is only stunned

It's natural for those who experience such a change to imagine that all sin is gone, completely rooted out of their heart, and it has no place there anymore. It's easy to conclude, "I feel no sin, therefore, I have none. It doesn't move, so it doesn't exist. It has no motion, so it has no being!"

But it's usually not long before they are undeceived. They find that sin was only suspended, not destroyed. Temptations return and sin revives, showing that it was only stunned before, not dead.

Now they feel two principles in themselves, plainly opposed to each other. The flesh is lusting against the spirit.[30] The old nature is fighting against the grace of God.[31]

On one hand, they still feel power to believe in Christ and to love God, and his Spirit still witnesses with their spirits that they are children of God.[32] On the other hand, they can't deny that sometimes they still feel in themselves pride or self-will or anger or unbelief. They often find one or more of these stirring in their heart, even if not taking control. These feelings may be pushing hard at them to make them fall. But they don't fall, because the Lord is their help.[33]

---

[30] *Live by the Spirit, I say, and do not gratify the desires of the flesh.* (Galatians 5:16)

[31] *But I see in my members another law at war with the law of my mind, making me captive to the law of sin that dwells in my members.* (Romans 7:23)

[32] *It is that very Spirit bearing witness with our spirit that we are children of God.* (Romans 8:16)

[33] *I was pushed hard, so that I was falling, but the Lord helped me.* (Psalm 118:13)

Fourteen hundred years ago, Macarius[34] exactly described this experience of the children of God:

> The unskillful (or inexperienced), when grace op-
> erates, presently imagine they have no more sin.
> Whereas they that have discretion cannot deny, that
> even we who have the grace of God may be molested
> again. For we have often had instances of some
> among the brethren, who have experienced such
> grace as to affirm that they had no sin in them; and
> yet, after all, when they thought themselves entirely
> freed from it, the corruption that lurked within was
> stirred up anew, and they were well nigh burned up.

What is sanctification?

From the time we are born again, the gradual work of sanctification takes place. We are enabled *by the Spirit* to *put to death
the deeds of the body,*[35] the deeds of our old evil nature. And as
we become more and more dead to sin, we become more and
more alive to God. We go on from grace to grace. This progress
keeps up just as long we are careful to *abstain from every form*

---

[34] There were several Christian writers named Macarius in the fourth century.
This quote is probably from Macarius of Egypt, who was admired by early
Methodists for his views on entire sanctification. (Based on research from
Wikipedia)

[35] *For if you live according to the flesh, you will die; but if by the Spirit you put to
death the deeds of the body, you will live.* (Romans 8:13)

of evil[36] and are *zealous for good deeds;*[37] as long as we do good to all people whenever we have an opportunity;[38] as long as we walk blamelessly in all God's laws, which is how we *worship in spirit and truth;*[39] as long as we take up our cross, and deny ourselves every pleasure that does not lead us closer to God.[40]

This is how we wait for entire sanctification, to be fully saved from all our sins of pride, self-will, anger, and unbelief. As the apostle expresses it, this is how we *go on to perfection.*[41]

But what is perfection? The word has various shades of meaning. Here it means perfect love.[42] It is love that allows no sin, love that fills the heart, taking up the whole capacity of the soul. It is love that always rejoices, never stops praying, and gives thanks in everything.[43]

---

[36] *Abstain from every form of evil.* (1 Thessalonians 5:22)

[37] *He it is who gave himself for us that he might redeem us from all iniquity and purify for himself a people of his own who are zealous for good deeds.* (Titus 2:14)

[38] *See that none of you repays evil for evil, but always seek to do good to one another and to all.* (1 Thessalonians 5:15 NRSV)

[39] *God is spirit, and those who worship him must worship in spirit and truth.* (John 4:24)

[40] *Then Jesus told his disciples, "If any want to become my followers, let them deny themselves and take up their cross and follow me."* (Matthew 16:24)

[41] *Therefore, leaving the discussion of the elementary principles of Christ, let us go on to perfection, not laying again the foundation of repentance from dead works and of faith toward God.* (Hebrews 6:1 NKJV)

[42] Wesley expands on this in his sermon "Christian Perfection," which is also available in the John Wesley in Modern Language series.

[43] *Rejoice in the Lord always; again I will say, Rejoice. Let your gentleness be known to everyone. The Lord is near. Do not worry about anything, but in everything by prayer and supplication with thanksgiving let your requests be made known to God.* (Philippians 4:4–6)

* * *

Discussion Questions

(1) The first two paragraphs imply that many people make religion much harder and more complicated than it should be. What is your experience of that?

(2) Before reading this, how would you have defined salvation?

— Has this chapter changed your thoughts any?

(3) Can you give examples from your own life of ways God drew you to him?

(4) If you can identify a time when you became saved, how does Wesley's description of the resulting peace, joy, and love fit your experience?

(5) "We feel this love producing love in us for every human being, and especially for the children of God."

— What is the difference between "every human being" and those who are "children of God"?

— John 1:12 says *But to all who received him, who believed in his name, he gave power to become children of God.* How does clarify the question?

— What are the implications of this in how you think about other people?

(6) How much do you identify with Wesley's description of your old nature fighting the grace of God in you?

(7) Is growing in holiness or sanctification something you consciously work toward?

— Why or why not?

2

What Do You Mean by Faith?

What is faith, through which we are saved? This is the second point to be considered.

Light and sight

Faith, in general, is defined by the author of Hebrews as a divine *evidence of things not seen*[44] — not visible, not able to be perceived by sight or any of the other external senses. It implies supernatural evidence both of God and of the things of God. The original Greek word can mean both evidence and conviction, which is the sense of being convinced by evidence. Faith is both a spiritual light exhibited to the soul, and a supernatural seeing or perception of that light. So the Scripture sometimes speaks of God giving light, and sometimes

---

[44] *Now faith is the substance of things hoped for, the evidence of things not seen.* (Hebrews 11:1 NKJV)

giving the power to see it.

For instance, St. Paul writes, *It is the God who said, "Let light shine out of darkness," who has shone in our hearts to give the light of the knowledge of the glory of God in the face of Jesus Christ.*[45] Elsewhere the same apostle speaks of the eyes of our understanding being opened.[46] By this double operation of the Holy Spirit, having the eyes of our soul both opened and enlightened, we see things which the natural *eye has not seen, nor ear heard.*[47] We have a view of the invisible things of God. We see the spiritual world, which is all around us, and yet as invisible to our natural senses as if it didn't even exist. And we see the eternal world, piercing through the veil which hangs between time and eternity. Clouds and darkness[48] cover it no more, but we already see the glory which shall be revealed in the future.[49]

Taking the word in a more particular sense, faith is a divine evidence and conviction not only that *in Christ God was*

---

[45] *For it is the God who said, "Let light shine out of darkness," who has shone in our hearts to give the light of the knowledge of the glory of God in the face of Jesus Christ.* (2 Corinthians 4:6)

[46] *The eyes of your understanding being enlightened; that you may know what is the hope of His calling, what are the riches of the glory of His inheritance in the saints,* (Ephesians 1:18 NKJV)

[47] *But, as it is written, "What no eye has seen, nor ear heard, nor the human heart conceived, what God has prepared for those who love him."* (1 Corinthians 2:9)

[48] *That day will be a day of wrath, a day of distress and anguish, a day of ruin and devastation, a day of darkness and gloom, a day of clouds and thick darkness.* (Zephaniah 1:15)

[49] *I consider that the sufferings of this present time are not worth comparing with the glory about to be revealed to us.* (Romans 8:18)

reconciling the world unto himself,[50] but also that Christ loved me personally, and gave himself for me. This is the faith by which we receive Christ in all his functions, as our Prophet,[51] Priest,[52] and King.[53] This is the faith by which he *became for us wisdom from God, and righteousness and sanctification and redemption.*[54]

Assurance and confidence

Someone asks, "But is this the faith based on an inner sense that we are saved, or the faith based on a decision to trust and follow Jesus?"

Scripture doesn't divide faith up that way. St. Paul says there is *one faith* and *one hope of your calling* — one Christian, saving faith — just as *there is one Lord* in whom we believe, and *one God and Father of all.*[55]

Clearly, this one faith necessarily implies an inner assurance

---

[50] *That is, in Christ God was reconciling the world to himself, not counting their trespasses against them, and entrusting the message of reconciliation to us.* (2 Corinthians 5:19)

[51] *When the people saw the sign that he had done, they began to say, "This is indeed the prophet who is to come into the world."* (John 6:14)

[52] *Since, then, we have a great high priest who has passed through the heavens, Jesus, the Son of God, let us hold fast to our confession.* (Hebrews 4:14)

[53] *On his robe and on his thigh he has a name inscribed, "King of kings and Lord of lords."* (Revelation 19:16)

[54] *He is the source of your life in Christ Jesus, who became for us wisdom from God, and righteousness and sanctification and redemption.* (1 Corinthians 1:30)

[55] *There is one body and one Spirit, just as you were called to the one hope of your calling, one Lord, one faith, one baptism, one God and Father of all, who is above all and through all and in all.* (Ephesians 4:4–6)

(which is here only another word for evidence) that Christ *loved me, and gave himself for me.*[56] For those who believe with the true living faith have the witness in themselves. The Holy Spirit witnesses with their spirit that they are a child of God. Because the believer is God's child, God has sent forth the Spirit of God's Son into their heart, crying, *"Abba, Father!"*[57]

This gives both an assurance of the believer's identity in Christ, and a childlike confidence in God. But notice that, by the very nature of the thing, assurance goes before confidence. For a person cannot have a childlike confidence in God until they know they are a child of God. Therefore, confidence, trust, reliance, adherence, or whatever else one wishes to call it is not the first sign of faith but the second.

This is the faith, taking that word in its highest sense, by which we are saved, justified, and sanctified.

But how are we justified and sanctified by faith? This is our third point of inquiry. And since this is the main point in question, and a point of more than ordinary importance, it is appropriate to consider it more closely.

* * *

---

[56] *And it is no longer I who live, but it is Christ who lives in me. And the life I now live in the flesh I live by faith in the Son of God, who loved me and gave himself for me.* (Galatians 2:20)

[57] *For you did not receive a spirit of slavery to fall back into fear, but you have received a spirit of adoption. When we cry, "Abba! Father!" it is that very Spirit bearing witness with our spirit that we are children of God.* (Romans 8:15–16)

Discussion Questions

(1) How is faith evidence? What is it evidence of?

(2) How does faith cause you to be convinced of something?

(3) Wesley says saving faith requires believing that God's work through Jesus was not only to love and save the world, but to love and save you personally.

— Why is this so hard for some people?

(4) What does the inner witness or assurance Wesley mentions feel like to you?

— How would you describe it?

(5) How much confidence do you have that God loves you as his child and will take care of you?

— What is that confidence based on?

3

The Faith That Makes Us Right With God

How are we justified by faith? What exactly do we mean by that? I answer, faith is the condition, and the only condition, of justification.

It is the condition, in that the only people who are justified are those who believe. Without faith no one is justified.[58]

And it is the only condition, because faith alone is sufficient for justification. Everyone who believes is justified, whether they have anything else or not.[59]

To say it another way: no one is justified until they believe, and everyone is justified when they believe.

---

[58] *And without faith it is impossible to please God, for whoever would approach him must believe that he exists and that he rewards those who seek him.* (Hebrews 11:6)

[59] *For by grace you have been saved through faith, and this is not your own doing; it is the gift of God.* (Ephesians 2:8)

Repentance and good deeds

Someone says, "But doesn't God command us to repent also? And to *bear fruit worth of repentance*?[60] To cease, for instance, from doing evil, and learn to do good? And aren't both faith and repentance completely necessary, to the point that if we willingly neglect either one, we can't reasonably expect to be justified at all? But if this is true, how can it be said that faith is the only condition of justification?"

God does indeed command us to repent,[61] and to act in ways that show our repentance.[62] If we willingly neglect these commands, we can't reasonably expect to be justified at all. Therefore, yes, both repentance and corresponding changes in our behavior are, in some sense, necessary to justification. But they are not necessary in the same way as faith, nor to the same degree.

Behavior that demonstrates repentance is not necessary to the same degree as faith, because it is only necessary if conditions allow; in other words, if there is time and opportunity. Otherwise, a person may be justified without it, as was the thief on the cross.[63] But a person cannot be justified

---

[60] *Bear fruit worthy of repentance.* (Matthew 3:8)

[61] *So they went out and proclaimed that all should repent.* (Mark 6:12)

[62] *But someone will say, "You have faith and I have works." Show me your faith apart from your works, and I by my works will show you my faith.* (James 2:18)

[63] *Then he said, "Jesus, remember me when you come into your kingdom." He replied, "Truly I tell you, today you will be with me in Paradise."* (Luke 23:42–43)

without faith. That is impossible.[64]

Likewise, a person can have all the repentance in the world, or all the good deeds. Still, that by itself isn't enough. That person is not justified until they believe. But the moment they believe, they are justified[65] — with or without those deeds, and with more or less repentance.

So repentance and corresponding actions are necessary to justification, but not to the same degree as faith. Nor are they necessary in the same way as faith is necessary. Repentance and corresponding behavior are only indirectly necessary, as results of faith. But faith is directly necessary to justification.

We are left with the fact that faith is the only condition which is immediately and directly necessary to justification.

How are we made holy?

The objection continues: "But do you believe we are sanctified by faith? We know you believe that we are justified by faith. But isn't it true that you both believe and teach that we are sanctified by our actions?"

For twenty-five years people have vehemently said this about me. But the fact is I have constantly declared, in every way I could, just the opposite. I have continually testified in private and in public that we are sanctified by faith as well as justified

---

[64] *And without faith it is impossible to please God, for whoever would approach him must believe that he exists and that he rewards those who seek him.* (Hebrews 11:6)

[65] *But to one who without works trusts him who justifies the ungodly, such faith is reckoned as righteousness.* (Romans 4:5)

by it.

Indeed, one of those great truths clearly illustrates the other. Exactly as we are justified by faith, in the same way are we sanctified by faith.[66]   Faith is the condition, and the only condition, of sanctification, exactly as it is of justification.[67] Faith is the condition: no one is sanctified except a person who has faith, and without faith no one is sanctified. And faith is the only condition, the only thing needed for sanctification: everyone who believes is sanctified, no matter what else they have or don't have. To put it another way, no one is sanctified until they believe, and everyone, when they believe, is sanctified.

Good deeds and repentance

"But isn't there a repentance after justification, as well as a repentance before it? And isn't it required that everyone who is justified be zealous of good deeds? Don't you yourself teach that this repentance and these works are so necessary that if a person willingly neglects them, they cannot reasonably expect to ever be sanctified in the full sense, that is, perfected in love? Don't you teach that such a person cannot grow at all in grace, in the loving knowledge of our Lord Jesus Christ; cannot even retain the grace God has already given them? Don't you teach that a

---

[66] *And this is what some of you used to be. But you were washed, you were sanctified, you were justified in the name of the Lord Jesus Christ and in the Spirit of our God.* (1 Corinthians 6:11)

[67] *To open their eyes so that they may turn from darkness to light and from the power of Satan to God, so that they may receive forgiveness of sins and a place among those who are sanctified by faith in me.* (Acts 26:18)

person who neglects these things cannot continue in the faith they received, or in the favor of God? But if all this is true, how can you say that faith is the only condition of sanctification?"

I do agree with all this, and I continually teach it as the truth of God. I agree there is a repentance after justification as well as before it.[68] It is indeed required that everyone who is justified be *zealous of good deeds.*[69] And yes, this repentance and these works are so necessary that if a person willingly neglects them, they cannot reasonably expect that they shall ever be sanctified. They cannot grow in grace, in the image of God, in the mind which was in Christ Jesus; they cannot retain the grace they have received; and they cannot continue in faith, or in the favor of God.

So what does all this show? Why, that both repentance, rightly understood, and the practice of all good works — works of religion and works of mercy (which we can now appropriately call them, since they spring from faith) — both of these are, in some sense, necessary to sanctification.

* * *

---

[68] *If we confess our sins, he who is faithful and just will forgive us our sins and cleanse us from all unrighteousness.* (1 John 1:9)

[69] *He it is who gave himself for us that he might redeem us from all iniquity and purify for himself a people of his own who are zealous for good deeds.* (Titus 2:14)

Discussion Questions

(1) If someone asked you how to be justified, what would you tell them?

(2) What is the clearest definition you have ever heard of the word "repentance?"

(3) Wesley's argument in the section called "Repentance and good deeds" can be confusing.

— What is he saying, in your own words?

(4) If someone asked you how to be sanctified, what would you tell them?

(5) Wesley says, "Everyone, when they believe, is sanctified." A few paragraphs later he says both repentance and good works "are, in some sense, necessary to sanctification."

— Is he contradicting himself?

— If not, how do you reconcile these statements?

4

Two Kinds of Repentence

I say "repentance rightly understood," because we must not confuse the kind of repentance that comes after justification with the repentance that goes before it.

The second kind of repentance

Repentance after we are justified is very different from the repentance that leads to justification. This repentance doesn't come from a sense of guilt or condemnation or an awareness of God's anger against sin. It doesn't mean we doubt God's favor or suffer any tormenting fear.[70]

Instead, this second kind of repentance might more accurately be described as a conviction worked in the soul by the

---

[70] *There is no fear in love; but perfect love casts out fear, because fear involves torment. But he who fears has not been made perfect in love.* (1 John 4:18 NKJV)

Holy Spirit.[71] It makes us aware of the sin which still remains in our heart — of the worldly mind, which "does still remain" (as the church liturgy says) "even in them that are born again," though it no longer has control over us. It's a reminder that we are prone to evil, that our heart wants to slide back into worldly ways, and that our flesh still continues to lust against the spirit.[72] Unless we continually *watch and pray*,[73] it lusts sometimes to pride, sometimes to anger, sometimes to love of the world, love of comfort, love of fame, or love of pleasure more than of God. This repentance is a conviction of the tendency of our heart to self-will, to ignoring God, or to the idolatry of valuing things higher than God. Above all is the tendency to unbelief that leads us in a thousand ways and under a thousand pretenses to continually move away, whether much or little, from the living God.

Along with this conviction of the sin remaining in our hearts is a clear conviction of the sin remaining in our lives, still attaching itself to everything we say and do. In the best of our expressions and actions we now discern a mixture of evil. Whether in our attitude or in the words or deeds themselves or in the way we say or do them, we find something that could not endure the righteous judgement of God, if he were to take note of every little thing we do wrong. Where we least suspected it, we find in ourselves a taint of pride or self-will, of unbelief or idolatry.

---

[71] *And when He has come, He will convict the world of sin, and of righteousness, and of judgment:* (John 16:8 NKJV)

[72] *But I see in my members another law at war with the law of my mind, making me captive to the law of sin that dwells in my members.* (Romans 7:23)

[73] *Take heed, watch and pray; for you do not know when the time is.* (Mark 13:33 NKJV)

The result is that we are now more ashamed of our best efforts than we used to be of our worst sins.[74] We can't help feeling that our deeds are so far from having anything of value in them, we are so far from being able to stand in the sight of divine justice, that God would hold us as guilty for these things as for actual sins, were it not for the atoning sacrifice of Jesus' blood.[75]

Experience shows that this kind of repentance implies a third thing, beyond the conviction of sin remaining in our hearts and attaching itself to all our words and actions, and beyond the guilt which that sin would bring on us if Christ were not continually sprinkling us with his atoning blood. The third thing implied in this repentance is a conviction of our helplessness. We are utterly unable to think one good thought or form one good desire, much less to speak one right word or perform one good action, except through God's free, almighty grace, first going ahead of us, and then accompanying us every moment.[76]

What kind of good deeds?

"But what exactly are those good deeds that you say are necessary to sanctification?"

---

[74] *The saying is sure and worthy of full acceptance, that Christ Jesus came into the world to save sinners—of whom I am the foremost.* (1 Timothy 1:15)

[75] *In this is love, not that we loved God but that he loved us and sent his Son to be the atoning sacrifice for our sins.* (1 John 4:10)

[76] *I am the vine, you are the branches. Those who abide in me and I in them bear much fruit, because apart from me you can do nothing.* (John 15:5)

First, all religious deeds. These include public prayer, family prayer, and praying in private; receiving the Lord's Supper; hearing, reading, and meditating on the Bible; and fasting to the extent that our bodily health allows.

Second, all deeds of mercy, whether they relate to the bodies or souls of those in need. These include feeding the hungry, clothing the naked, entertaining the stranger, and visiting those who are in prison, or sick, or are afflicted in other ways.[77] They also include efforts to instruct the ignorant, to awaken the unaware sinner, to motivate the lukewarm, to strengthen the wavering, to comfort the weak, to encourage the tempted, or to contribute in any other way to the saving of souls from death.

This is the repentance, and these are the *fruits worthy of repentance*,[78] which are necessary to full sanctification. This is the way God has appointed for his children to wait for complete salvation.

---

[77] *Then the righteous will answer him, "Lord, when was it that we saw you hungry and gave you food, or thirsty and gave you something to drink? And when was it that we saw you a stranger and welcomed you, or naked and gave you clothing? And when was it that we saw you sick or in prison and visited you?" And the king will answer them, "Truly I tell you, just as you did it to one of the least of these who are members of my family, you did it to me."* (Matthew 25:37–40)

[78] *Bear fruits worthy of repentance. Do not begin to say to yourselves, "We have Abraham as our ancestor;" for I tell you, God is able from these stones to raise up children to Abraham.* (Luke 3:8)

Don't block sanctification

So we can see how extremely harmful is the seemingly innocent idea which some teach that there is no sin in a believer; that all sin is destroyed, root and branch, the moment a person is justified. This notion completely blocks up the way to sanctification, because it totally prevents repentance after justification. There is no place for repentance in a person who believes they have no sin in their life or their heart. Consequently, it becomes impossible for such a person to become perfected in love, because repentance is absolutely necessary for that.

We can also see that there is no possible danger in expecting full salvation — expecting to grow beyond being justified to being made completely holy in this life. Even if we're mistaken, even if no such blessing ever was or can be attained, we still don't lose anything. In fact, that very expectation motivates us to use all the talents God has given us, indeed, to become more skillful in all of them, so that when our Lord comes, he will receive his own with interest.[79]

Only faith

But to return to the main point: even though both this second kind of repentance and its appropriate deeds are necessary to

---

[79] *Then you ought to have invested my money with the bankers, and on my return I would have received what was my own with interest.* (Matthew 25:27)

full salvation, yet they are not necessary either in the same way as faith, or to the same degree.

The deeds are not necessary in the same degree because they are only necessary conditionally, if there is time and opportunity for them. Otherwise a person may be sanctified without them. But one cannot be sanctified without faith.

In the same way, no matter how much of this repentance a person has, or how many good deeds, it's not enough; they are not sanctified until they believe. But the moment they believe, with or without those deeds and with more or less of this repentance, they are sanctified.

And this repentance and these deeds are not necessary in the same way as faith, because they are only indirectly necessary. They are necessary to remain in faith and to grow in it. But faith is immediately and directly necessary for sanctification.

So we see that faith is the only condition which is immediately and directly necessary for sanctification.

* * *

Discussion Questions

(1) For some people, repenting for the old life and turning to God to become a Christian is a very emotional experience. For others it is more of a decision of the will, or something they more or less grew into.

— What was your experience?

(2) Wesley makes a distinction between the kind of repentance required to become a Christian and the kind of repentance required for wrong things we say or do after becoming Christians. How are they different?

(3) If a non-Christian asked you what the Bible means by "sin," what would you tell them?

(4) Wesley talks about sin remaining in our hearts, and sin remaining in our lives. Explain the difference and give examples.

(5) How much encouragement and opportunity does your church provide for doing good works?

— Works of religion?

— Works of mercy?

— How could your church improve in these areas?

(6) Does Wesley's argument in the last section sound familiar?

— Where in this sermon did he say something similar?

— Why do you think he so closely repeated it?

5

The Faith That Makes Us Holy

The objector continues: "But what is that faith by which we are sanctified; by which we are saved from sin and perfected in love?"

It is a divine evidence and conviction of three things.

God's promise

First, saving faith is a divine evidence and conviction that God has promised sanctification in the holy scripture. Until we are thoroughly convinced of this, we cannot move one step further.

You would think a reasonable person would not need any more to convince them of this than the ancient promise:

> *The Lord your God will circumcise your heart and the heart of your descendants, so that you will love the Lord your God with all your heart and with all your soul, in*

order that you may live.[80]

How clearly this describes being perfected in love! How strongly it implies being saved from all sin! Because as long as love fills up the whole heart, what room is there in it for sin?

God's ability

Second, this faith is a divine evidence and conviction that God is able to do what he promised.

We admit that for mortals it is impossible to bring a clean thing out of an unclean, to purify the heart from all sin, and to fill it with all holiness. But human inability is not a problem, because for God all things are possible. Surely no one ever imagined that it was possible to any power less than that of the Almighty! But if God speaks, it shall be done. God says, "Let there be light," and there is light!

God's willingness

Third, this faith is a divine evidence and conviction that God is able and willing to do it now.

And why not? Isn't a moment to God the same as a thousand

---

[80] *Moreover, the Lord your God will circumcise your heart and the heart of your descendants, so that you will love the Lord your God with all your heart and with all your soul, in order that you may live.* (Deuteronomy 30:6)

years? He doesn't need more time to accomplish whatever is his will. And he doesn't need to wait for any more worthiness or fitness in the persons he is pleased to honor. So we can boldly say, at any point of time, Now is the day of salvation! Today, if you hear His voice, do not harden your hearts! Look, I have prepared my dinner. Come to the wedding banquet!

God's action

We need to add one more thing to this confidence that God is both able and willing to sanctify us now: a divine evidence and conviction that he does it. At that moment it is done.

God says to the inmost soul, *Let it be done for you according to your faith.*[81] At that moment the soul is made pure from every spot of sin. It is clean from all unrighteousness.[82] And the believer experiences the deep meaning of those solemn words, *If we walk in the light as he himself is in the light, we have fellowship with one another, and the blood of Jesus his Son cleanses us from all sin.*[83]

---

[81] *And to the centurion Jesus said, "Go; let it be done for you according to your faith." And the servant was healed in that hour.* (Matthew 8:13)

[82] *If we confess our sins, he who is faithful and just will forgive us our sins and cleanse us from all unrighteousness.* (1 John 1:9)

[83] *But if we walk in the light as he himself is in the light, we have fellowship with one another, and the blood of Jesus his Son cleanses us from all sin.* (1 John 1:7)

How soon can I get it?

"But does God work this great work in the soul gradually or instantly?"

Perhaps it may be worked gradually in some people, or at least they can't pinpoint the particular moment when sin ceased to be. But it's so much better, when it's the will of God, that it should be done instantly; that the Lord should destroy sin *by the breath of his mouth,*[84] *in a moment, in the twinkling of an eye.*[85] And this is the way he generally does it — a plain fact, of which there is evidence enough to satisfy any unprejudiced person.

So look for it every moment! Look for it in the way described above, in finding yourself doing all those good works for which you are created anew in Christ Jesus.[86] There's no danger; you can't be worse for that expectation, even if you're no better. For even if you were to be disappointed of that hope, still you don't lose anything.

But you won't be disappointed.[87] Your hope will come, and

---

[84] *And then the lawless one will be revealed, whom the Lord Jesus will destroy with the breath of his mouth, annihilating him by the manifestation of his coming.* (2 Thessalonians 2:8)

[85] *In a moment, in the twinkling of an eye, at the last trumpet. For the trumpet will sound, and the dead will be raised imperishable, and we will be changed.* (1 Corinthians 15:52)

[86] *For we are what he has made us, created in Christ Jesus for good works, which God prepared beforehand to be our way of life.* (Ephesians 2:10)

[87] *And hope does not disappoint us, because God's love has been poured into our hearts through the Holy Spirit that has been given to us.* (Romans 5:5)

will not tarry.[88] Look for it then every day, every hour, every moment! Why not this hour, this moment? Certainly you may look for it now, if you believe it comes by faith.

And this is how to know for sure whether you are seeking it by faith or hoping to earn it by your works. If you're trusting in your good works, then you look for something you have to do first, before you can be sanctified. You think, "I must first be or do this or that." If that's you, you are still seeking to earn your sanctification by works.

But if you seek to be sanctified by faith, you can expect it to happen just the way you are, and you can expect it now.

It's important to observe that there is an inseparable connection between these three points: expect it by faith; expect it as you are; and expect it now! To deny one of them, is to deny them all; to allow one, is to allow them all.

Don't wait for anything

Do you believe we are sanctified by faith? Then be true to your belief, and look for this blessing just as you are, neither better nor worse; as a poor sinner that has nothing to pay with, nothing to claim, but "Christ died."

And if you look for it as you are, then expect it now. Don't wait for anything. Why should you? Christ is ready, and he is all you need.

---

[88] *For there is still a vision for the appointed time; it speaks of the end, and does not lie. If it seems to tarry, wait for it; it will surely come, it will not delay.* (Habakkuk 2:3)

He is waiting for you. He is at the door![89] Let your inmost soul cry out,

> Come in, come in, thou heavenly Guest!
>   Nor hence again remove;
>   But sup with me, and let the feast
>   Be everlasting love.[90]

* * *

Discussion Questions

(1) How willing are you to believe and base your actions on promises from God that you read in the Bible?

— Why?

(2) How do the statements in the section called "God's ability" fit with popular teaching about human potential, self-help, and positive thinking?

— Which do you trust more?

---

[89] *Listen! I am standing at the door, knocking; if you hear my voice and open the door, I will come in to you and eat with you, and you with me.* (Revelation 3:20)

[90] This is a version of the last verse from Charles Wesley's hymn, "Come, Let Us Who in Christ Believe."

(3) Many people believe God is able to answer a prayer or do a good thing, but they have trouble believing God wants to do it for them.

— Why do you think this is?

— What is the solution?

(4) What is Wesley saying in the section called "God's action?"

— How do we put that into practice?

(5) In the first part of the subsection titled "How soon can I get it?" Wesley says "there is evidence enough to satisfy any unprejudiced person" that instant sanctification is "the way [God] generally does it."

— What evidence is he referring to?

— Do you think there was more of this kind of evidence in Wesley's day than today?

— Why?

(6) Wesley tells us "how to know for sure whether you are seeking [sanctification] by faith or hoping to earn it by your works." How do you score on that test?

(7) If you don't feel that you are already entirely sanctified, are you willing to pray expectantly to receive it right here and now?

(8) Extra credit! If you found this book worthwhile, help others find it by leaving a brief review wherever you bought it.

6

Appendix: Wesley's Original Words

The Scripture Way of Salvation

By John Wesley

Sermon #43, first published in 1771. This version from *The Works of John Wesley*, Third American Edition, 1872, edited by Thomas Jackson.

Ye are saved through faith. — Ephesians 2:8

1. Nothing can be more intricate, complex, and hard to be understood, than religion, as it has been often described. And this is not only true concerning the religion of the Heathens, even many of the wisest of them, but concerning the religion of those also who were, in some sense, Christians; yea, and men of great name in the Christian world; men who seemed to be pillars thereof. Yet how easy to be understood, how plain and simple a thing, is the genuine religion of Jesus Christ; provided only

that we take it in its native form, just as it is described in the oracles of God! It is exactly suited, by the wise Creator and Governor of the world, to the weak understanding and narrow capacity of man in his present state. How observable is this, both with regard to the end it proposes, and the means to attain that end! The end is, in one word, salvation; the means to attain it, faith.

2. It is easily discerned, that these two little words, I mean faith and salvation, include the substance of all the Bible, the marrow, as it were, of the whole Scripture. So much the more should we take all possible care to avoid all mistake concerning them, and to form a true and accurate judgement concerning both the one and the other.

3. Let us then seriously inquire,

I. What is Salvation?
  II. What is that faith whereby we are saved? And,
  III. How are we saved by it?

1. And, first, let us inquire, What is salvation? The salvation which is here spoken of is not what is frequently understood by that word, the going to heaven, eternal happiness. It is not the soul's going to paradise, termed by our Lord, "Abraham's bosom." It is not a blessing which lies on the other side death; or, as we usually speak, in the other world. The very words of the text itself put this beyond all question: "Ye are saved." It is not something at a distance: it is a present thing; a blessing which, through the free mercy of God, ye are now in possession of. Nay, the words may be rendered, and that with equal propriety, "Ye have been saved": so that the salvation which is here spoken of

might be extended to the entire work of God, from the first dawning of grace in the soul, till it is consummated in glory.

2. If we take this in its utmost extent, it will include all that is wrought in the soul by what is frequently termed "natural conscience," but more properly, "preventing grace"; — all the drawings of the Father; the desires after God, which, if we yield to them, increase more and more; —all that light wherewith the Son of God "enlighteneth every one that cometh into the world;" showing every man "to do justly, to love mercy, and to walk humbly with his God"; —all the convictions which His Spirit, from time to time, works in every child of man—although it is true, the generality of men stifle them as soon as possible, and after a while forget, or at least deny, that they ever had them at all.

3. But we are at present concerned only with that salvation which the Apostle is directly speaking of. And this consists of two general parts, justification and sanctification. Justification is another word for pardon. It is the forgiveness of all our sins; and , what is necessarily implied therein, our acceptance with God. The price whereby this hath been procured for us (commonly termed "the meritorious cause of our justification"), is the blood and righteousness of Christ; or, to express it a little more clearly, all that Christ hath done and suffered for us, till He "poured out His soul for the transgressors." The immediate effects of justification are, the peace of God, a "peace that passeth all understanding," and a "rejoicing in hope of the glory of God"with joy unspeakable and full of glory."

4. And at the same time that we are justified, yea, in that very moment, sanctification begins. In that instant we are born

again, born from above, born of the Spirit: there is a real as well as a relative change. We are inwardly renewed by the power of God. We feel "the love of God shed abroad in our heart by the Holy Ghost which is given unto us"; producing love to all mankind, and more especially to the children of God; expelling the love of the world, the love of pleasure, of ease, of honor, of money, together with pride, anger, self-will, and every other evil temper; in a word, changing the earthly, sensual, devilish mind, into "the mind which was in Christ Jesus."

5. How naturally do those who experience such a change imagine that all sin is gone; that it is utterly rooted out of their heart, and has no more any place therein! How easily do they draw that inference, "I feel no sin; therefore, I have none: it does not stir; therefore it does not exist: it has no motion; therefore, it has no being!"

6. But it is seldom long before they are undeceived, finding sin was only suspended, not destroyed. Temptations return, and sin revives; showing it was but stunned before, not dead. They now feel two principles in themselves, plainly contrary to each other; "the flesh lusting against the Spirit"; nature opposing the grace of God. They cannot deny, that although they still feel power to believe in Christ, and to love God; and although His "Spirit" still "witnesses with their spirits, that they are children of God"; yet they feel in themselves sometimes pride or self-will, sometimes anger or unbelief. They find one or more of these frequently stirring in their heart, though not conquering; yea, perhaps, "thrusting sore at them that they may fall"; but the Lord is their help.

7. How exactly did Macarius, fourteen hundred years ago,

describe the present experience of the children of God: "The unskilful," or unexperienced, "when grace operates, presently imagine they have no more sin. Whereas they that have discretion cannot deny, that even we who have the grace of God may be molested again. For we have often had instances of some among the brethren, who have experienced such grace as to affirm that they had no sin in them; and yet, after all, when they thought themselves entirely freed from it, the corruption that lurked within was stirred up anew, and they were wellnigh burned up."

8. From the time of our being born again, the gradual work of sanctification takes place. We are enabled "by the Spirit" to "mortify the deeds of the body," of our evil nature; and as we are more and more dead to sin, we are more and more alive to God. We so on from grace to grace, while we are careful to "abstain from all appearance of evil," and are "zealous of good works," as we have opportunity, doing good to all men; while we walk in all His ordinances blameless, therein worshipping Him in spirit and in truth; while we take up our cross, and deny ourselves every pleasure that does not lead us to God.

9. It is thus that we wait for entire sanctification; for a full salvation from all our sins, —from pride, self-will, anger, unbelief; or, as the Apostle expresses it, "go unto perfection." But what is perfection? The word has various senses: here it means perfect love. It is love excluding sin; love filling the heart, taking up the whole capacity of the soul. It is love "rejoicing evermore, praying without ceasing, in everything giving thanks."

II. But what is faith through which we are saved? This is the second point to be considered.

1. Faith, in general, is defined by the Apostle, *O pragmaton elenchos ou blepomenon*. An evidence, a divine evidence and conviction (the word means both) of things not seen; not visible, not perceivable either by sight, or by any other of the external senses. It implies both a supernatural evidence of God, and of the things of God; a kind of spiritual light exhibited to the soul, and a supernatural sight or perception thereof. Accordingly, the Scripture speaks of God's giving sometimes light, sometimes a power of discerning it. So St. Paul: "God, who commanded light to shine out of darkness, hath shined in our hearts, to give us the light of the knowledge of the glory of God in the face of Jesus Christ." And elsewhere the same Apostle speaks of "the eyes of" our "understanding being opened." By this two-fold operation of the Holy Spirit, having the eyes of our soul both opened and enlightened, we see the things which the natural "eye hath not seen, neither the ear heard." We have a prospect of the invisible things of God; we see the spiritual world, which is all round about us, and yet no more discerned by our natural faculties than if it had no being. And we see the eternal world; piercing through the veil which hangs between time and eternity. Clouds and darkness then rest upon it no more, but we already see the glory which shall be revealed.

2. Taking the word in a more particular sense, faith is a divine evidence and conviction not only that "God was in Christ, reconciling the world unto Himself," but also that Christ loved me, and gave Himself for me. It is by

42

this faith (whether we term it the essence, or rather a property thereof) that we receive Christ; that we receive Him in all His offices, as our Prophet, Priest, and King. It is by this that He is "made of God unto us wisdom, and righteousness, and sanctification, and redemption."

3. "But is this the faith of assurance, or faith of adherence?" The Scripture mentions no such distinction. The Apostle says, "There is one faith, and one hope of our calling"; one Christian, saving faith; "as there is one Lord," in whom we believe, and "one God and Father of us all." And it is certain, this faith necessarily implies an assurance (which is here only another word for evidence, it being hard to tell the difference between them) that Christ loved me, and gave Himself for me. For "he that believeth" with the true living faith "hath the witness in himself": "the Spirit witnesseth with his spirit that he is a child of God."Because he is a son, God hath sent forth the Spirit of His Son into his heart, crying, Abba, Father"; giving him an assurance that he is so, and a childlike confidence in Him. But let it be observed, that, in the very nature of the thing, the assurance goes before the confidence. For a man cannot have a childlike confidence in God till he knows he is a child of God. Therefore, confidence, trust, reliance, adherence, or whatever else it be called, is not the first, as some have supposed, but the second, branch or act of faith.

4. It is by this faith we are saved, justified, and sanctified; taking that word in its highest sense. But how are we justified and sanctified by faith? This is our third head of inquiry. And this being the main point in question, and a point of no ordinary importance, it will not be improper

to five it a more distinct and particular consideration.

III.

1. And, first, how are we justified by faith? In what sense is this to be understood? I answer, Faith is the condition, and the only condition, of justification. It is the condition: none is justified but he that believes: without faith no man is justified. And it is the only condition: this alone is sufficient for justification. Every one that believes is justified, whatever else he has or has not. In other words: no man is justified till he believes; every man when he believes is justified.

2. "But does not God command us to repent also? Yea, and to 'bring forth fruits meet for repentance'—to cease, for instance, from doing evil, and learn to do well? And is not both the one and the other of the utmost necessity, insomuch that if we willingly neglect either, we cannot reasonably expect to be justified at all? But if this be so, how can it be said that faith is the only condition of justification?" God does undoubtedly command us both to repent, and to bring forth fruits meet for repentance; which if we willingly neglect, we cannot reasonably expect to be justified at all: therefore both repentance, and fruits meet for repentance, are, in some sense, necessary to justification. But they are not necessary in the same sense with faith, nor in the same degree. Not in the same degree; for those fruits are only necessary conditionally; if there be time and opportunity for them. Otherwise a man may be justified without them, as was the thief upon the cross (if we may call him so; for a late writer has discovered that he was no thief, but a very honest and respectable person!); but he cannot be justified without faith; this is impossible. Likewise, let a man have ever so much repentance, or ever so many of the fruits meet for

repentance, yet all this does not at all avail; he is not justified till he believes. But the moment he believes, with or without those fruits, yea, with more or less repentance, he is justified. —Not in the same sense; for repentance and its fruits are only remotely necessary; necessary in order to faith; whereas faith is immediately necessary to justification. It remains, that faith is the only condition, which is immediately and proximately necessary to justification.

3. "But do you believe we are sanctified by faith? We know you believe that we are justified by faith; but do not you believe, and accordingly teach, that we are sanctified by our works?" So it has been roundly and vehemently affirmed for these five-and-twenty years: but I have constantly declared just the contrary; and that in all manner of ways. I have continually testified in private and in public, that we are sanctified as well as justified by faith. And indeed the one of those great truths does exceedingly illustrate the other. Exactly as we are justified by faith, so are we sanctified by faith. Faith is the condition, and the only condition, of sanctification, exactly as it is of justification. It is the condition: none is sanctified but he that believes; with out faith no man is sanctified. And it is the only condition: this alone is sufficient for sanctification. Every one that believes is sanctified, whatever else he has or has not. In other words, no man is sanctified till he believes: every man when he believes is sanctified.

4. "But is there not a repentance consequent upon, as well as a repentance previous to, justification? And is it not incumbent on all that are justified to be 'zealous of good works'? Yea, are not these so necessary, that if a man willingly neglect them he cannot reasonably expect that he shall ever be sanctified in the full sense; that is, perfected in love? Nay, can he grow at all in

grace, in the loving knowledge of our Lord Jesus Christ? Yea, can he retain the grace which God has already given him? Can he continue in the faith which he has received, or in the favor of God. Do not you yourself allow all this, and continually assert it? But, if this be so, how can it be said that faith is the only condition of sanctification?"

5. I do allow all this, and continually maintain it as the truth of God. I allow there is a repentance consequent upon, as well as a repentance previous to, justification. It is incumbent on all that are justified to be zealous of good works. And there are so necessary, that if a man willingly neglect them, he cannot reasonably expect that he shall ever be sanctified; he cannot grow in grace, in the image of God, the mind which was in Christ Jesus; nay, he cannot retain the grace he has received; he cannot continue in faith, or in the favor of God. What is the inference we mist draw herefrom? Why, that both repentance, rightly understood, and the practice of all good works, —works of piety, as well as works of mercy (now properly so called, since they spring from faith), are, in some sense, necessary to sanctification.

6. I say, "repentance rightly understood"; for this must not be confounded with the former repentance. The repentance consequent upon justification is widely different from that which is antecedent to it. This implies no guilt, no sense of condemnation, no consciousness of the wrath of God. It does not suppose any doubt of the favor of God, or any "fear that hath torment." It is properly a conviction, wrought by the Holy Ghost, of the sin which still remains in our heart; of the _phronEma sarkos_, the carnal mind, which "does still remain" (as our Church speaks) "even in them that are regenerate"; although it does no longer reign; it has not now dominion over

46

them. It is a conviction of our proneness to evil, of an heart bent to backsliding, of the still continuing tendency of the flesh to lust against the spirit. Sometimes, unless we continually watch and pray, it lusteth to pride, sometimes to anger, sometimes to love of the world, love of ease, love of honor, or love of pleasure more than of God. It is a conviction of the tendency of our heart to self-will, to Atheism, or idolatry; and above all, to unbelief; whereby, in a thousand ways, and under a thousand pretenses, we are ever departing, more or less, from the living God.

7. With this conviction of the sin remaining in our hearts, there is joined a clear conviction of the sin remaining in our lives; still cleaving to all our words and actions. In the best of these we now discern a mixture of evil, either in the spirit, the matter, or the manner of them; something that could not endure the righteous judgement of God, were He extreme to mark what is done amiss. Where we least suspected it, we find a taint of pride or self-will, of unbelief or idolatry; so that we are now more ashamed of our best duties than formerly of our worst sins: and hence we cannot but feel that these are so far from having anything meritorious in them, yea, so far from being able to stand in sight of the divine justice, that for those also we should be guilty before God, were it not for the blood of the covenant.

8. Experience shows that, together with this conviction of sin remaining in our hearts, and cleaving to all our words and actions; as well as the guilt which on account thereof we should incur, were we not continually sprinkled with the atoning blood; one thing more is implied in this repentance; namely, a conviction of our helplessness, of our utter inability to think one good thought, or to form one good desire; and much more to speak one word aright, or to perform one good action, but

through His free, almighty grace, first preventing us, and then accompanying us every moment.

9. "But what good works are those, the practice of which you affirm to be necessary to sanctification?" First, all works of piety; such as public prayer, family prayer, and praying in our closet; receiving the supper of the Lord; searching the Scriptures, by hearing, reading, meditating; and using such a measure of fasting or abstinence as our bodily health allows.

10. Secondly, all works of mercy; whether they relate to the bodies or souls of men; such as feeding the hungry, clothing the naked, entertaining the stranger, visiting those that are in prison, or sick, or variously afflicted; such as the endeavoring to instruct the ignorant, to awaken the stupid sinner, to quicken the lukewarm, to confirm the wavering, to comfort the feeble-minded, to succor the tempted, or contribute in any manner to the saving of souls from death. This is the repentance, and these the "fruits meet for repentance," which are necessary to full sanctification. This is the way wherein God hath appointed His children to wait for complete salvation.

11. Hence may appear the extreme mischievousness of that seemingly innocent opinion, that there is no sin in a believer; that all sin is destroyed, root and branch, the moment a man is justified. By totally preventing that repentance, it quite blocks up the way to sanctification. There is no place for repentance in him who believes there is no sin either in his life or heart: consequently, there is no place for his being perfected in love, to which that repentance is indispensably necessary.

12. Hence it may likewise appear, that there is no possible danger in thus expecting full salvation. For suppose we were mistaken, suppose no such blessing ever was or can be attained, yet we lose nothing: nay, that very expectation quickens us in

using all the talents which God has given us; yea, in improving them all; so that when our Lord cometh, He will receive His own with increase.

13. But to return: Though it be allowed, that both this repentance and its fruits are necessary to full salvation; yet they are not necessary either in the same sense with faith, or in the same degree: —Not in the same degree; for these fruits are only necessary conditionally, if there be time and opportunity for them; otherwise a man may be sanctified without them. But he cannot be sanctified without faith. likewise, let a man have ever so much of this repentance, or ever so many good works, yet all this does not at all avail: he is not sanctified till he believes. But the moment he believes, with or without those fruits, yea, with more or less of this repentance, he is sanctified. —Not in the same sense; for this repentance and these fruits are only remotely necessary, — necessary in order to the continuance of his faith, as well as the increase of it; whereas faith is immediately and directly necessary to sanctification. It remains, that faith is the only condition which is immediately and proximately necessary to sanctification.

14. "But what is that faith whereby we are sanctified, —saved from sin, and perfected in love?" It is a divine evidence and conviction, first, that God hath promised it in the holy Scripture. Till we are thoroughly satisfied of this, there in no moving one step further. And one would imagine there needed not one word more to satisfy a reasonable man of this, than the ancient promise, "Then will I circumcise thy heart, and the heart of thy seed, to love the Lord they God with all thy heart, and with all thy soul, and with all thy mind." How clearly does this express the being perfected in love! —how strongly imply the being saved from all sin! For as long as love takes up the whole heart,

what room is there for sin therein?

15. It is a divine evidence and conviction, secondly, that what God hath promised He is able to perform. Admitting, therefore, that "with men it is impossible" to "bring a clean thing out of an unclean," to purify the heart from all sin, and to till it with all holiness; yet this creates no difficulty in the case, seeing "with God all things are possible." And surely no one ever imagined it was possible to any power less than that of the Almighty! But if God speaks, it shall be done. God saith, "Let there be light; and there" is "light"!

16. It is, thirdly, a divine evidence and conviction that He is able and willing to do it now. And why not? Is not a moment to Him the same as a thousand years? He cannot want more time to accomplish whatever is His will. And He cannot want or stay for any more worthiness or fitness in the persons He is pleased to honor. We may therefore boldly say, at any point of time, "Now is the day of salvation!"To-day, if ye will hear His voice, harden not your hearts!"Behold, all things are now ready; come unto the marriage!"

17. To this confidence, that God is both able and willing to sanctify us now, there needs to be added one thing more, —a divine evidence and conviction that He doeth it. In that hour it is done: God says to the inmost soul, "According to thy faith be it unto thee!" Then the soul is pure from every spot of sin; it is clean "from all unrighteousness." The believer then experiences the deep meaning of those solemn words, "If we walk in the light as He is in the light, we have fellowship one with another, and the blood of Jesus Christ His Son cleanseth us from all sin."

18. "But does God work this great work in the soul gradually or instantaneously?" Perhaps it may be gradually wrought in some; I mean in this sense, —they do not advert to the particular

moment wherein sin ceases to be. But it us infinitely desirable, were it the will of God, that it should be done instantaneously; that the Lord should destroy sin "by the breath of His mouth," in a moment, in the twinkling of an eye. And so He generally does; a plain fact, of which there is evidence enough to satisfy any unprejudiced person. Thou therefore look for it every moment! Look for it in the way above described; in all those good works whereunto thou art "created anew in Christ Jesus." There in then no danger: you can be no worse, if you are no better, for that expectation. For were you to be disappointed of your hope, still you lose nothing. But you shall not be disappointed of your hope: it will come, and will not tarry. Look for it then every day, every hour, every moment! Why not this hour, this moment? Certainly you may look for it now, if you believe it is by faith. And by this token you may surely know whether you seek it by faith or by works. If by works, you want something to be done first, before you are sanctified. You think, I must first be or do thus or thus. Then you are seeking it by works unto this day. If you seek it by faith, you may expect it as you are; and expect it now. It is of importance to observe, that there is an inseparable connection between these three points, - -expect it by faith; expect it as you are; and expect it now! To deny one of them, is to deny them all; to allow one, is to allow them all. Do you believe we are sanctified by faith? Be true then to your principle; and look for this blessing just as you are, neither better nor worse; as a poor sinner that has still nothing to pay, nothing to plead, but "Christ died." And if you look for it as you are, then expect it now. Stay for nothing: why should you? Christ is ready; and He is all you want. He is waiting for you: He is at the door! Let your inmost soul cry out,

Come in, come in, thou heavenly Guest!

51

Nor hence again remove;
But sup with me, and let the feast
Be everlasting love.

About the Author

Best known internationally as author of *Pastoring: The Nuts and Bolts*, in print in seven languages, David Wentz has a passion for helping people connect with God and make a difference. Combining 38 years as a pastor with a first career in engineering and graduate degrees from three very different seminaries (charismatic, mainstream, and Wesleyan-evangelical), he expresses God's truth in ways everyone can appreciate.

Raised in the Episcopal church, Dr. Wentz has also been part of Nazarene, Pentecostal Holiness, and non-denominational congregations. As a Methodist pastor he served small, large, and multicultural churches in rural, small-town, suburban, and urban settings, served as a regional church consultant in the Maryland – D.C. area, and led workshops for pastors internationally. In 2015 he retired to the rural Ozarks, where he writes, works in God's great outdoors, and oversees Doing

Christianity, Inc., a small non-profit devoted to equipping pastors in developing and minority-Christian countries.

In 1974, David married his college sweetheart, Paula. They have five children with wonderful spouses, and fourteen grand-children.

The book of Ezekiel describes David's calling. Twenty-five hundred years ago God called Ezekiel to teach God's ways and proclaim the Holy Spirit, who revives dry bones and forms them into a dwelling for God and a source of living water that heals nations.

Bones are still dry today. God still wants to dwell among his people. Nations still need healing. And people still need to be taught God's ways and be moved by God's Spirit. That's what David calls "Doing Christianity."

You can connect with me on:

🌐 https://www.pastordavidwentz.com

📘 https://www.facebook.com/profile.php?id=100064901162331

Subscribe to my newsletter:

✉️ https://mailchi.mp/c162e27f817b/doing-christianity-email-newsletter-sign-up

Also by David Wentz

Christianity is about more than just going to heaven when you die. It's about becoming like Jesus and living the Kingdom of God in this life. That not only blesses us, it blesses everyone around. That's what I call doing Christianity, and it's what my books are all about.

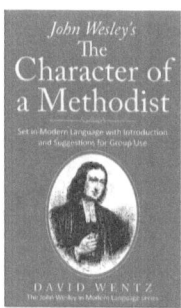

John Wesley's "The Character of a Methodist:" Set in Modern Language with Introduction and Suggestions for Group Use
A perennial best-seller since its publication, this summary of the root emphases of Wesley's teaching is required reading in today's turbulent times. Father of Methodism and grandfather of Pentecostalism and the Salvation Army, Wesley shows the character of a true Christian of any denomination. Part of the John Wesley in Modern Language series.

John Wesley's "The New Birth:" Set in Modern Language with Introduction and Suggestions for Group Use

Is being good the way to heaven? Being religious? Jesus said, "You must be born again. John Wesley explains Jesus' words in this brief classic. One of the standard sermons Wesley required his circuit riders to learn and re-preach, *The New Birth* shows that religion and morality are good but new life in Jesus is vital. Part of the John Wesley in Modern Language series.

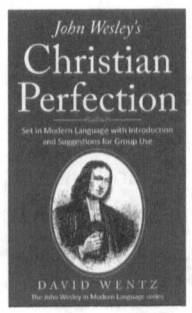

John Wesley's "Christian Perfection:" Set in Modern Language with Introduction and Suggestions for Group Use

"Christians aren't perfect, just forgiven." John Wesley doesn't agree. Christians not only can become perfect in this life — God commands us to!

Seeking perfection was an integral part of the explosive growth of Methodism for 100 years, even as it led to the persecution of those who practiced it. It's time to recover that power. Part of the John Wesley in Modern Language series.

"This book thrilled my soul and reinvigorated my hope." — Amazon reviewer

When Church Stops Working: Meeting With God in Your Living Room

If you ever led a meeting or taught a class, you and your friends can be a fully functioning part of God's work in the world.

For pastors, here's a proven way to extend your reach by mentoring living-room church leaders and networks.

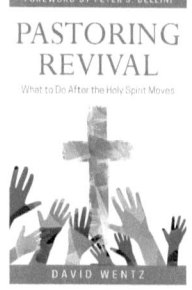

Pastoring Revival: What to Do After the Holy Spirit Moves

"Come, Holy Spirit!" Then what? Few pastors are trained what to do if God answers with unusual power. Drawing on two fascinating case studies, academic research, and his own thirty-eight years as a pastor, seeker, and student of revival, Dr. Wentz has produced a practical, engaging, Biblical, actionable guide to prepare every pastor for the next great move of God.

"It's hard to put to words how excited this book makes me. I have pastored for years . . . Read this book, and get ready." — Amazon reviewer

Pastoring: The Nuts and Bolts — Options and Best Practices for Leading a Church

Crossing denominations and cultures and solidly grounded in Scripture, *Pastoring* offers options and best practices instead of dogmatic assertions. It moves from God's purpose for the church to the pastor's personal life, then covers worship, preaching, leadership, administration, and issues relevant to charismatic and Pentecostal churches not normally addressed in this kind of book. In seven languages and counting, *Pastoring* has blessed thousands of new and seasoned pastors.